TAROT FOR BEGINNERS

The Ultimate Tarot Reading Guide for Beginners

(How to Survive as a Tarot Reader)

Kimberly Seifert

Published by Sharon Lohan

© **Kimberly Seifert**

All Rights Reserved

Tarot for Beginners: The Ultimate Tarot Reading Guide for Beginners (How to Survive as a Tarot Reader)

ISBN 978-1-990334-70-2

All rights reserved. No part of this guide may be reproduced in any form without permission in writing from the publisher except in the case of brief quotations embodied in critical articles or reviews.

Legal & Disclaimer

The information contained in this book is not designed to replace or take the place of any form of medicine or professional medical advice. The information in this book has been provided for educational and entertainment purposes only.

The information contained in this book has been compiled from sources deemed reliable, and it is accurate to the best of the Author's knowledge; however, the Author cannot guarantee its accuracy and validity and cannot be held liable for any errors or omissions. Changes are periodically made to this book. You must consult your doctor or get professional medical advice before using any of the suggested remedies, techniques, or information in this book.

Upon using the information contained in this book, you agree to hold harmless the Author from and against any damages, costs, and expenses, including any legal fees potentially resulting from the application of any of the information provided by this guide. This disclaimer applies to any damages or injury caused by the use and application, whether directly or indirectly, of any advice or information presented, whether for breach of contract, tort, negligence, personal injury, criminal intent, or under any other cause of action.

You agree to accept all risks of using the information presented inside this book. You need to consult a professional medical practitioner in order to ensure you are both able and healthy enough to participate in this program.

Table of Contents

INTRODUCTION 1

CHAPTER 1: ADVANCED SPREADS 6

CHAPTER 2: VARIETIES OF TAROT DECKS 33

CHAPTER 3: HISTORY OF TAROT 40

CHAPTER 4: HOW TO USE TAROT CARDS 57

CHAPTER 5: TAROT – AN INSIGHT 63

CHAPTER 6: LEARNING TO READ TAROT CARDS 67

CHAPTER 7: INTERPRETING THE CARDS AND CLOSING THE READING 76

CHAPTER 8: INTERPRETING THE HIDDEN MEANINGS OF PATTERNS(INCLUDING THE CELTIC CROSS SPREAD) 82

CHAPTER 9: THE STUDY OF MINOR ARCANA 92

CHAPTER 10: PENTACLES 103

CHAPTER 11: TAROT SPELLS AND RITUALS 119

CHAPTER 12: TAROT SPREADS 133

CHAPTER 13: TOP TEN MYTHS ABOUT TAROT CARDS AND TAROT READING 144

CONCLUSION 160

Introduction

In our society, tarot reading is among those subjects that are considered taboo. Whether it is out of ignorance, or the need to fit in a certain group of people who are "too smart" and self-confident to believe in this "complete nonsense"; those who want to will always find a reason to avoid the need to face reality. Yes, reality is not only what we can see with our eyes: it includes the people, objects, phenomena, and the entire natural world around us.

There is also the reality of our unconscious selves: certain forces, perspectives, ways of thinking, and motivations that are triggered by a certain factor in our past that can influence our present choices / desires / decisions. You might be wondering why I chose this introduction for my book. To be honest, I felt the urge to show that tarot reading is not just a "bunch of cards" that were chosen "by chance", by a person who is too weak to find a solution to his/ her problems. Or that the reader is just a charlatan who wants to make money by telling stories.

This is probably the most common interpretation that those lacking the minimum knowledge about this practice tend to make. Sigmund Freud, the father of psychoanalysis, was the first to present the role of our unconscious in our present desires and fears for the future, but also in the actions that we make without really understanding why. This theory was later developed by many other important theorists (Lacan and Jung being just two of them).

Thus, half of the problem is explained. Then comes the part where we try to make sense of the way in which the reader can actually interpret the meaning of our (unconscious) choices. How could a simple card with a drawing on it reflect my life? And how does the reader know what that refers to? Well, this is why the best answers can be given by professional and experienced readers, who have both the theoretical knowledge and the past sessions to rely on. Over time, they have developed an interpretation style of their own, which is influenced by the person in front of them and by the signs on each card. It is not something occult, but it's definitely on a "more" metaphysical level.

But, am I saying that only old and experienced tarot readers are reliable? Absolutely not. Every person has to start somewhere. Although there are people with stronger vibrations, who have a better ability to "read" the person in front of them, there is no such thing as a born tarot reader. So how does anyone start in this art? It was observed that, from the oldest times of tarot reading, people tended to react in similar ways to the cards. As the archetypal theory tells us, humans are connected through a sort of collective unconsciousness, and this is why we respond or perceive certain external factors in the same way. These archetypes can vary from culture to culture, but overall, they all have the same basis. This is how, over centuries, certain meanings were attributed to each of the cards.

I can imagine that so much information can be hard to take in at one time. So let me use another method to explain what tarot reading really is - by saying what tarot reading is NOT:

What the cards show you does not necessarily need or have to happen

Tarot reading is not the devil's tool nor can it be labeled as "witchcraft"

No occult rituals have to be made in order to get the right results

You or any tarot reader are not psychics if you practice it (much less witches)

There is no special way in which you must procure your cards (for instance, given as a gift from a special person or inherited)

The power is not in a specific deck of cards; the power will belong to you/ the tarot reader and will be influenced by the seeker

The cards are not always right.

All these are popular myths about the practice of tarot reading. I will present them and many others in the following chapter, stating their possible source and the truth behind them.

So keep reading in order to understand the history of tarot reading. Many essential details are waiting for you to become a master in this technique. Thus, clear your mind and get prepared for the science behind tarot reading.

Chapter 1: Advanced Spreads

These spreads usually use a lot of cards and will most likely require that you use the minor arcana cards, too. Some sets of cards only come with the major, but to get a more clear answer to the question, you'll want to use a set with both the major and the minor arcana.

Annikin Career

The annikin career spread examines someone's underlying reasons for choosing a particular career path or job. It will help them figure out whether or not they chose the correct path and what obstacles may be in their way when it comes to progressing.

The Spread

1   2   3   4   5

Card 1: Why those chose their career.

Card 2: If they're on the correct path.

Card 3: What main obstacles they're facing.

Card 4: What is in their favor.

Card 5: How can they move forward?

Annikin Finance

The Annikin finance spread tells the inquirer their financial situation and what they should be concerned about and if anything can be done to improve their security.

The Spread

1	10	7

8	9

5	6

2	3	4

Card 1: What are their concerns about money?

Card 2: What are their concerns about money?

Card 3: What are their concerns about money?

Card 4: What are their concerns about money?

Card 5: How can they obtain financial security?

Card 6: How can they obtain financial security?

Card 7: How can they obtain financial security?

Card 8: Who can they receive help from?

Card 9: Who can they receive help from?

Card 10: What are their plans for the future?

Annikin Work

The annikin work spread describes someone's career or job and whether they made the right choice.

The Spread

1   2   3

Card 1: Did they choose the right career?

Card 2: Is the career secure?

Card 3: Should they make changes or go?

Annual

The annual card spread looks at only the next twelve months and the thirteenth card represents the overall feel for the year. You can expand this one using twenty-four cards for each month and get a feel for how each day of the month will go.

The Spread

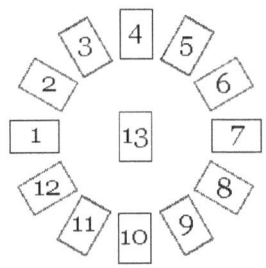

Card 1: January

Card 2: February

Card 3: March

Card 4: April

Card 5: May

Card 6: June

Card 7: July

Card 8: August

Card 9: September

Card 10: October

Card 11: November

Card 12: December

Card 13: Overall Feel For The Year

Celtic Cross

The Celtic cross spread is one used to answer a specific question the inquirer has.

The Spread

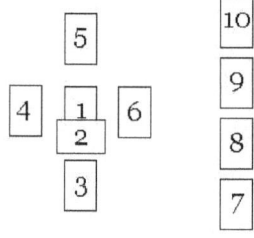

Card 1: What influences are around the inquirer?

Card 2: Are there any obstacles around the inquirer and what are they?

Card 3: The past that created the current situation.

Card 4: The distant past the person has to deal with.

Card 5: What the inquirer wants to achieve.

Card 6: The future.

Card 7: The attitude on the matter.

Card 8: How others view the inquirer.

Card 9: The inquirer's hopes and fears.

Card 10: The outcome.

Checking The Direction

This spread is all about the inquirer's life and where it's heading. There are trends shown and tips and hints that the inquirer and use to avoid pitfalls.

The Spread

1   7

2   6

3   5

4

Card 1: The past.

Card 2: The present.

Card 3: The future.

Card 4: Tips for the inquirer.

Card 5: Tips and suggestions for the inquirer.

Card 6: Obstacles that must be avoided or overcome.

Card 7: The outcome.

Child

The child spread is about what the inquirer's child was put on this earth for. It tells them their purpose.

The Spread

1   2

5   6   7

3   4

Card 1: What they came to learn.

Card 2: Where they are now.

Card 3: Where they shine.

Card 4: What the inquirer needs to know about the child.

Card 5: Where they are going in the next couple of years.

Card 6: Something that will impact the child in a negative or positive way.

Card 7: What the child will achieve.

Childhood Problems

This spread is about the inquirer's child and if there is something major going on to change the child's behavior. If there isn't any negative behavior, the spread will indicate possible future behaviors that might be unsavory.

The Spread

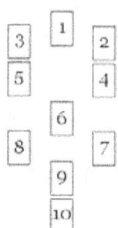

Card 1: If there is a problem with the child.

Card 2: What happened in the past to make the child this way.

Card 3: Present influences that are affecting the current problem.

Card 4: How can the problem be resolved.

Card 5: The outcome.

Card 6: Are there going to be any problems in the future?

Card 7: What will the problem be connected to?

Card 8: Can anything be done to prevent the problem?

Card 9: How can the problem be helped when it does occur?

Card 10: The outcome.

Is He / She The One?

Sometimes we just don't know who might be the one for us, so we turn to the cards to understand. This spread is about answering the question most people are asking when they're in a relationship, is that person that one?

The Spread

3   1   4

2

5   7   6

Card 1: Is this person the one?

Card 2: Will there be a commitment or marriage in the future?

Card 3: Negative influences in the relationship.

Card 4: Positive influences in the relationship.

Card 5: What can the inquirer do in order to become ready for the person to join their life?

Card 6: What does the person need to do before they can join the inquirer's life?

Card 7: Will the inquirer be happy with the person they're inquiring about?

Is It Too Late?

Many of us ask this question when we're in a relationship that doesn't seem to be working or we've recently broken up with someone that we really thought it would work out with. This spread will answer that question once and for all.

The Spread

1	3	6
5	7	9
2	4	8

Card 1: The inquirer's position in the relationship.

Card 2: The inquirer's ex-partner's position in the relationship.

Card 3: Positive actions that can be taken by the inquirer.

Card 4: Negative actions that they shouldn't take.

Card 5: Other influences that may shape the situation that are positive or negative.

Card 6: The amount of time it may take for the reunion to take place.

Card 7: The amount of success in the short-term.

Card 8: The degree of success in the long-term.

Card 9: The overall recommendation in the situation.

Mirror-Mirror

The mirror-mirror spread is all about what both partners need to do in order for them to improve their relationship and what their wants and needs are.

The Spread

1   2

3   4

5   6

7   8

9   10

11   12

13   14

Card 1: How the inquirer views themselves.

Card 2: How the partner views the inquirer.

Card 3: How the inquirer sees the relationship.

Card 4: How the partner sees the relationship.

Card 5: What the inquirer wants.

Card 6: What the partner wants.

Card 7: What the inquirer needs.

Card 8: What the partner needs.

Card 9: Positive influences of the inquirer.

Card 10: Negative influences of the inquirer.

Card 11: Positive influences of the partner.

Card 12: Negative influences of the partner.

Card 13: What the inquirer needs to do.

Card 14: What the partner needs to do.

Mountains and Molehills

This spread will tell the inquirer what present and future complications will plague them and whether or not they will be a minor or a major complication. These complications can relate to emotional, physical, and spiritual complications.

The Spread

1		4		7		10	
2			3		5		6
8		9		11		12	

Card 1: The spiritual challenge.

Card 2: The minor spiritual challenge.

Card 3: The minor Spiritual Challenge.

Card 4: The main emotional challenge.

Card 5: The minor emotional challenge.

Card 6: The minor emotional challenge.

Card 7: The major mental challenge.

Card 8: The minor mental challenge.

Card 9: The minor mental challenge.

Card 10: The major challenge.

Card 11: The minor spiritual challenge.

Card 12: The minor spiritual challenge.

Tree Of Life

The tree of life spread refers to the inquirer's present situation and looks at their emotional, spiritual, home, family, and career circumstances. It also looks at their responsibilities and any obstacles and help that they might find.

The Spread

1

3   2

5   4

6

8   7

9

10

Card 1: Spiritual circumstance.

Card 2: Responsibilities.

Card 3: Challenges.

Card 4: Helpful occurrences.

Card 5: Opposing occurrences.

Card 6: Achievements.

Card 7: Emotional relationships.

Card 8: Communiqué and career.

Card 9: Foundation.

Card 10: Family and home.

Which Job?

When it comes to our career, sometimes choosing the right path might seem difficult, especially if there's more than one decision. Ideally, the inquirer will have more than one job they are looking at, most likely two.

The Spread

1

2   3

4   7

5   6   8   9

Card 1: What is the inquirer searching for in a job?

Card 2: What is positive about job A that the inquirer likes?

Card 3: What is positive about job B the inquirer likes?

Card 4: What is the attraction of job A?

Card 5: What is the benefit to job A?

Card 6: What is the negative of job A?

Card 7: What is the positive of job B?

Card 8: What is the benefit of job B?

Card 9: What is the negative of job B?

Which Love?

This spread actually does not determine who the inquirer should love, but who they love that they should spend time with. If they believe they're in love with two people, then they are not in love with either person and are not ready for a relationship. But if they have two people that could become a potential lover, they need to choose who they should spend time with.

The Spread

1   6

2   3   4   7
8   9

5   10

Card 1: Does the inquirer's first choice have the potential to become a true love?

Card 2: Things that might be an obstacle to the relationship with the first choice.

Card 3: Influences that might be in favor of the relationship with the first choice.

Card 4: What can the inquirer do to make the first choice a part of their life?

Card 5: Will they be happy with their first choice?

Card 6: Does the second choice have the potential to become a true love?

Card 7: Things that might be a negative or an obstacle for the second choice.

Card 8: Things that might be in favor for the relationship with the second choice.

Card 9: What can the inquirer do to make the second choice a part of their life?

Card 10: Will the inquirer be happy with the second choice?

Stuck

If you are the inquirer are feeling stuck with a problem or in life, then this spread will look at the state of main areas in your or the inquirer's life and consider what can be done to improve the complication.

The Spread

1

```
2         3         4         5
6         7    8
9         10        11        12
13        14        15
16
```

Card 1: The overall feel of the inquirer's life.

Card 2: Current state of the family affairs.

Card 3: Current state of friendships.

Card 4: Current state of love.

Card 5: Current state of financial status.

Card 6: Current state of the inquirer's career.

Card 7: Current emotions about their physical location.

Card 8: Current state of their spirituality.

Card 9: What can be done to improve the family relationships.

Card 10: What can be done to improve the friendships.

Card 11: What can be done to improve love.

Card 12: What can be done to improve money.

Card 13: What can be done to improve their career.

Card 14: What can be done to improve their location.

Card 15: What can be done to improve their spirituality.

Card 16: The outcome of any of the changes that are made.

Sibling Rivalry

Sometimes we have children that are in the midst of a sibling rivalry, but we're not sure what their part in the rivalry is and how we may have played a part in it. This spread is designed to help answer the question of what the first and second child's problems are and what the parent or guardian can do in order to make the situation better. It also addresses what part the guardian may be playing in the situation.

The Spread

1	2	3
4	5	6
7	8	9

Card 1: How the first child sees the second child.

Card 2: The first child's part in the complication.

Card 3: The inquirer's part in the problem regarding the first child.

Card 4: How the second child sees the first child.

Card 5: The second child's part in the complication.

Card 6: The inquirer's part in the complication regarding the second child.

Card 7: What the inquirer needs to do in regards to the first child.

Card 8: What the inquirer needs to do with regards to the second child.

Card 9: Will the situation get better?

Ongoing Relationship

In an ongoing relationship, we may need to look at where our relationship is going to head in the future. This spread is designed to give the answer to that question.

The Spread

1

2   3

4   5   6

7   8   9   10

Card 1: The past of the relationship.

Card 2: The inquirer's past experiences in the relationship.

Card 3: The inquirer's partner's past experiences in the relationship.

Card 4: The inquirer's current experiences in the relationship.

Card 5: The inquirer's partner's present experiences in the relationship.

Card 6: The present relationship status.

Card 7: What the inquirer can expect in the future.

Card 8: What the partner may expect in the future.

Card 9: Where the relationship is heading as a whole.

Card 10: The outcome.

Money Problems

It's not uncommon for people to go to a tarot card reader because they want to know about their current money situation. This spread will look at their present financial situation and what they can do in order to make it better.

The Spread

1

2   3

4   5

6

Card 1: The cause of the problem.

Card 2: What the inquirer has to do.

Card 3: Negative aspects working against the inquirer.

Card 4: Positive aspects working with the inquirer.

Card 5: Who can help them?

Card 6: The outcome.

Missing Pet

If you or someone's pet has gone missing, this spread can be used to find the pet or tell the person what happened to the pet.

The Spread

1	2	
3	4	5
6	7	8
9		

Card 1: The pet that is missing.

Card 2: Something that the inquirer should know about the loss.

Card 3: Where the inquirer should begin their search.

Card 4: Where the inquirer should begin their search.

Card 5: Where the inquirer should begin their search.

Card 6: Something that will help with the search.

Card 7: Someone who can help.

Card 8: Other things that should be considered.

Card 9: The outcome.

Chakra Balance

The chakra balance spread lets an inquirer know if their chakras are balanced and which ones they may need to work on.

The Spread

7

6

5

4

3

2

1

Card 1: The Root Chakra.

Card 2: The Spleen Chakra.

Card 3: The Solar Plexus Chakra.

Card 4: The Heart Chakra.

Card 5: The Throat Chakra.

Card 6: The Third-Eye Chakra.

Card 7: The Crown Chakra.

Chapter 2: Varieties Of Tarot Decks

Frankly, there are tons of different varieties of tarot decks and there is no official tarot decks used anywhere. A lot of them are similar, but there are those that have a lot of striking differences in theme and imagery. With that said, we are only going to list down the top most famous and essential tarot decks.

Rider-Waite Tarot

This is a classic among all the classics in tarot decks, also the most famous. This widely circulated deck is also known as Rider Tarot, Waite Tarot and Waite-Smith Tarot. It doesn't matter if you're a beginner or an expert in tarot reading, this deck should be added to your collection. This deck is available in multiple formats like miniature, pocket, standard and giant. The cards in this deck may not have the most colorful and extravagant designs, but that doesn't make them any less good than the latest tarot decks. Many people forget extravagant designs, but the classic are forever remembered. The creators of this deck are A. E. Waite and Pamela Colman-Smith.

Aleister Crowley Thoth Tarot

This deck has amazing artwork and is also considered as a classic tarot deck. Thoth Tarot deck contains 80 cards that includes three different versions of the card Magus. Also known as Crowley Thoth Tarot and Toth Tarot. A fine and classic deck indeed, but it is one of the darkest and most controversial card deck. Mainly because of the reputation of the cards creator, an occultist and a Golden Dawn member named Aleister Crowley. Take note that this tarot deck wasn't made for beginners. A lot has found this deck quite complex, due to the immeasurable amount of archetypal symbols.

Shadowscapes Tarot

This tarot deck is a must for all those fantasy lovers out there. Each card is endowed with stunning images and the watercolors added more to the mythical sight. Shadowscape follows the Rider-Waite theme, it even comes with a book. The designs are inspired by folklore, fantasy and nature. Fans and enthusiasts waited six long years before this tarot card deck made its debut. The most noticeable and appreciated in this tarot deck's design is the fact that everything is painted in a way that gives it the illusion of fluid motion. Hands down to the artists Stephanie Pui-Mun Law on her card designs.

Deviant Moon Tarot

What makes Deviant Moon Tarot is its design. Each card is surreal, unique and sometime quite disturbing. A borderless edition is available and a white booklet comes with the deck. You see, the theme is all about cemeteries and mental asylums, it kind of gives the users a sneak peek into the deepest and darkest part of their sub consciousness. Patrick Valenza, the creator, really put the dark and mystery into the twisted forms of nightmares and the elements of death. All the figures in the deck are nonhuman, the colors are gloomy and a lot of small details has something to do with the creator's childhood and imagination.

DruidCraft Tarot

From the name of the tarot deck itself, it's obvious that the drawings are based on Druidry and nature spiritualties. Also, as you guessed, it has a lot of nature elements into it. Just by looking at the tarot deck, you might even see the movement of the characters alongside their calm background. Keep in mind that there is a little nudity involved on both male and female, but that doesn't mean that they look any less attractive. It's amazing to think how brilliant Stephanie Carr-Gomm, Philip Carr-Gomm and Will Worthington were when they created DruidCraft Tarot and another tarot deck called Druid Animal Oracle.

Legacy of the Divine Tarot

You can't go wrong with the name, everything about this deck is simply divine and amazing. Not only are the designs rich, but also the color and ideas. Don't be afraid to own this deck if you're not a tarot expert, because it won't matter. Looking at each magical scene, all the details really to pop up since each one has a highly realistic and digital design. You really got to hand it to the artist, graphic designer and creator Ciro Marchetti. Though he has very little experience and background when it comes to tarot cards, he still managed to design a deck that didn't deviate too much from the original ideas.

Wild Unknown Tarot

A tarot deck that focused on nature, wild animals, symbolism and a lot of black and white. There are only a few splashes of color on each card, but that doesn't mean that it lacked beauty. If it was possible, the lack of color gave it even more beauty. Each line in every card can speak for themselves. This kind of theme and design is so unique that it would be a crime not to have in your collection, it's also one of the reason why it's popular. The creator, Kim

Krans, really put a lot of thought into each stroke and small details.

Victorian Romantic Tarot

This tarot deck is based on the engravings from the artists of the 19**th** century. Historical and the Victorian era are the main themes of this deck. When you look at the 78 cards on this tarot deck, you will be transported back in time. It's filled with everything concerning the Victorian passions and medieval styles. The creators Alex Ukolov and Karen Mahony sought to put various women from different levels in society; from the queen to the poor. Not only that, but there are intricate images and engravings scattered all over the cards.

Gaian Tarot

Gaian Tarot is solely dedicated to the earth, nature and Gaia herself. Before, this deck was only available as majors-only set until the minors were completed. This tarot deck is very traditional, from the number of cards to most of the titles and more. All the designs are so down-to-earth, they show communities interacting with nature and with each other. Not to mention tons of compilation of intricate designs and interpretative work. It's a fresh break from all the kings and queens of most of the tarot decks, better thank creator Joanna Powell Colbert for that.

Chapter 3: History Of Tarot

There are countless theories about the origins of tarot. Some scholars claim that the cards came from ancient Egypt. Others that present day Milan and Bologna can also be the birthplace of this art.

The Tarot has been in Europe since the 14th century. The first deck we are aware of in Europe was in Milan. It dates back to the 14th century. There are also theories connecting these cards to the Islamic cultures and even to India. Because the symbols on the cards are quite universal, the scholars cannot seem to agree about the origins of Tarot. They existed in different cultures throughout history. But many scholars agree that the cards most likely traveled from the East to the West.

Even the name Tarot, and its source are still a mystery. Some say the word derived from the German "tarock." Others believe it derived from the Italian word "tarocco" which means "blood orange." Some believe it comes from the Arabic "turuq" which means "ways." Others claim it came from the Egyptian origin "tar" and "ro" meaning the "royal road." Hebrews believe it derives from the word "Torah," the first five books of the Old Testament.

Tarot finds its roots in occultism. Today, the interest in them has expanded this tradition. The cards are often used by individuals from all walks of life. They all have one thing in common: A quest for a higher perspective. The process involves a person who is seeking for answers and a reader who is interpreting the cards.

Tarot cards are not meant to be used as a means for fortune telling. They have a much bigger purpose than that, and their energy should be handled for advice and help only. Tarot is a way for us to reflect back into ourselves and our lives. We use them for guidance. When asking a question we should avoid futuristic ones like "When will I get married?" or "How many kids will I have?" or "When will I find true love?" etc. Instead, we should focus on more specific like "Will I have a boy or a girl or both?" or "Will my spouse support me in my career change or should I stay where I am now?" or "Is there a way to improve my relationship at the moment?". Yes or no questions also work as they open pathways to a more in-depth reading.

TAROT DECKS

Hundreds, if not thousands of tarot decks are available today. Because these cards are personal, each user chooses the deck that speaks to him/her the most. After all, to interpret these symbols, we need to feel connected to them. In other words, they should touch our soul. It does not matter whether you are an absolute beginner or a seasoned expert. You need to feel a personal connection with them. We will talk more about how to choose the right deck later.

Just as the symbols are different, the number of cards in each deck is also different. Some of them have 16 cards; some have 22, 35 and some have 78 cards.

In most traditional decks there are 22 trump cards in the major arcana and 56 cards in the minor arcana. These 56 cards are divided into four different suits: wands, swords, coins and cups. There are also countless ways to spread them. Some of these spreads only use the major arcana; some only use the minor arcana and some use both.

The most popular themes are mythology, astrology, and angels. Aliens, Gothic, fantasy, history, Native American, religious, psychic, nature, and steampunk are also popular. But, to give you a better perspective, we will talk about a few of them.

Rider-Waite-Smith

The most popular one in the world. It is also one of the oldest decks. This deck is also easy to use for all beginners because of its imagery. And it is even easier to find resources on how to use them. The deck has 78 cards, 22 of which are the trumps or major arcana and 56 minor arcana cards with four suits. Each suit uses 14 cards. We will talk in detail about this deck in the

next chapter.

Tarot de Marseille

This deck is also known as Tarot of Marseille or Tarot de Marseilles. Italians first used it, and they carried it to

Southern France where the deck got its name. 78 cards, 22 of which are the trumps or major arcana and 56 minor arcana cards with four suits. The imagery takes its roots from Christianity. It also has controversial Christian images like a female pope.

Thoth Tarot Deck

This deck has 78 cards. Also, knows as Crowley Thoth Deck, it has kabbalistic and astrological symbols. Alistair Crowley describes these cards in his book titled "The Book of Thoth."

Gaian Tarot

This deck takes its influence from nature itself. With 78 cards, it is the reinterpretation of the classic Rider-Waite-Smith. But with a more spiritual, nature-oriented design. The Empress has become the Gardener, and the Magician is the new ritual drummer.

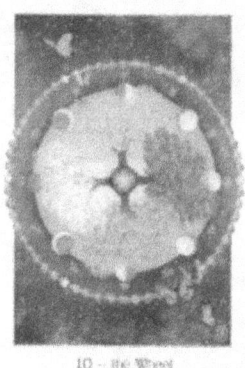

10 -- the Wheel

Fairy Tale Tarot

Another deck built following the footsteps of the classic Rider-Waite. This deck has a more magical, fairy tale-like design that takes you to a faraway place.

The Mythic Tarot

This set was first published in 1986. It comes with 78 cards and takes influence from the Greek mythological gods, goddesses, heroes, and heroines.

Tarocco Piemontese

This deck takes its origins from Italy. It is another version of the Tarot de Marseille. This one also consists of 78 cards with 22 trump cards and 56 minor arcana cards. The Fool has 0 as its number, and the rest of the major arcana cards go from 1 to 21. The minor arcana cards go from 2 to 10. Each suit's first card is its number 1. That card demonstrates the symbol of the corresponding suit in detail. Each suit also has a king, a queen, a knight and jack just like in the Rider-Waite deck.

Buddha Tarot

This is a non-traditional deck consisting of 79 cards with one extra trump card. The cards take inspiration from the story of Siddhartha and his journey towards enlightenment. Suits are Vajras, Double Vajras, Lotuses, and Jewels. The minor arcana has 56 cards.

XIX. Buddha & Sakti – The Sun

Shapeshifter Tarot

Another non-traditional deck that comes with a total of 81 cards. Lisa Hunt illustrated these cards with esoteric, mythological and pagan symbols. The set also has roots in paganism. Shape-shifting is taking the shape of an animal during trance. Celtic mythology inspires the idea of the shapeshifting concept of these cards. It focuses on the intuitive connection between nature, animals, and humans. The major arcana has 24 cards, and the minor arcana has 57.

Fifth Tarot

This deck is a more cosmic one aiming to illustrate the universal energy of the 5th dimension. It has an extra suit that called the Lost Suit and it represents ether. Out of 92 cards, 22 are majors and 70 are minors.

Osho Zen Tarot

This deck is inspired by the transcendental game Zen, and it has 79 cards. There is one extra card for Osho. The four suits are fire, clouds, rainbows and water. They have a spiritual design that suits intermediate to professional tarot readers better. Especially if they also have psychic abilities.

WHERE TO GET YOUR CARDS AND WHICH SET TO CHOOSE?

Choosing your first tarot deck as a beginner can be overwhelming. Considering the learning process takes time and practice. In general, we group the decks in two categories. There are cards with people doing something, and cards with symbols only. The second group is more numerology, Kabbalah, and mysticism oriented. The first group takes its roots from the traditional Raider-Waite Smith style cards.

The most important step in making a decision is to concentrate on your needs and what you want to use these cards for. Take your background and interests into account as well. If you are a beginner, you may find that the cards in the second group might not be easy to use in the learning process. Traditional cards might be a good first choice.

Depending on where you live, you might not have access to visit a tarot store. You might not see them in person and explore their symbols and imagery. In this case, you can go online and research your options. You will find a lot of websites that display each set in detail. You will be able to choose the set that speaks to you the most this way.

When you believe you have found the right deck for yourself, the next step is the quality of it. Some cards are thinner than normal to keep the costs low. If you are considering tarot reading for a long haul, choose a set that has heavier cards so they last longer. Many of these sets also come with a book that explains how to interpret the cards. They teach some common spreads that we use often.

The cards also come in different sizes. Some people prefer bigger ones, and some prefer smaller ones that they can carry with them at all times. It all depends on what you want to use these cards for. Whether it is personal or professional. You may find it easy to carry mini tarot cards in your purse or your bag. Maybe for more professional readings you would prefer bigger ones. Anyway, it is not forbidden to use several decks.

It is still possible to find tarot decks in local bookstores. These are usually the traditional Rider-Waite- Smith decks since it is the most popular. But the internet gives us more options today. There is an ocean of possibilities when it comes to tarot, and you will find a deck that suits your needs. You will be able to order online even if you cannot buy it direct from a local store. Thanks to the internet, people also notice the wide variety of styles. It makes tarot all the more enjoyable and convenient for those who are passionate about it.

REMEMBER that you must pick only the brand new decks so that afterward they will be charged with your energy and cards won't lie.

Chapter 4: How To Use Tarot Cards

Are you looking forward to visiting a tarot reader whereby you could drop your concerns like a hot rod and instantly receive a cooling solution in exchange? Well, visiting a tarot reader with your concerns may be a great idea, but if you are looking for a hands off procedure, where the tarot reader is singularly going to murmur a few words in total darkness and then tell you how to make your problems vanish, you surely have the wrong idea.

Tarot readers are not fortune tellers – surprised? Well, don't be. They are not soothsayers in any form. However, they are very good at helping you come to terms with your inner and higher self, the place where, essentially, all important information about your wellbeing lies. Even the sages of the Hermetic Order of the Golden Dawn, that 19th century organization that dealt with the paranormal, believed that your inner self was the richest place you could tap information from. And if all you need to know is within you, then you can see the logic in the assertion that you can do tarot reading fine even without being a psychic.

How to use your tarot cards

You have basically two options, all simple to use. Here they are:

Make use of questions

And here there is the temptation to think you could somewhat magically get an answer to a question like, say, should you drop your teaching career and take on nursing. Yet that is not what happens. As alluded to earlier, you have a role to play in making decisions pertaining to your life. So, you need to frame your questions right in order to benefit from tarot reading.

How to handle tarot questioning:

Make your questions open

What this means is that you need not ask what the legal fraternity calls leading questions. For instance, if you are concerned about your teenage child's career path, do not ask what you could do to influence your child to take accountancy as it pays well; rather ask what you could do to help your child choose a suitable career for his or her future. In short, when your question, kind of carries your anticipated answer, you are rendering your tarot cards useless. Do you want the cards to guide you? Then refrain from bringing your preconceived ideas to the questioning session.

Give just enough detail

Let your inquiry have some focus. That way, you can easily get an answer that targets your real concern. This is as opposed to making your question so detailed that it becomes difficult to identify the source of your problem. And even with focus, there also needs to be that broad outlook to the problem.

You could, for instance, ask how you could bring a balance between family time and recreation. On the contrary, it would not be very helpful for you to inquire the best way to co-ordinate your schedules for badminton, dance sessions, piano and family time. Those narrowed down details are not helpful. You want a less hectic life and your first question of balancing family life with recreation is sufficient.

Maintain the right focus

Have you realized how easy it is to address the role of someone else while really what you want to know is what you can do to have the problem solved? If, for instance, you are concerned that your son has become rebellious, you could ask what part you have played in enabling that behavior. But if you ask why your son has turned out to be rebellious, the tarot reading may not be very helpful as far as your problem is concerned.

Let your questions be neutral

This is to say that you need to avoid asking a question as though you would like the answer to lean towards a certain end; or like you are being accusatory. For instance, you could ask what you need to do to have your boss understand your situation better rather than ask why your boss does not seem to understand that you have good reason to be late for work every morning.

Let your question convey your positive attitude

It is helpful when you frame your question in a manner that shows you are ready to do your part to improve the situation or to solve the problem. On the contrary, it is not advisable to pose questions wondering why things are happening or not happening or why they are happening in a certain way and not another.

You can make open tarot readings

Here you do not provide any guidance as to your need to the tarot reader; no questions. Even if you are reading the tarots personally, you need to use your cards with an open mind. This type of tarot reading happens to be most helpful when you are looking at an open unknown future. Instances when you could use open tarot reading is when you are about to begin married life; begin a fresh career; you have just graduated; and so on.

Chapter 5: Tarot – An Insight

Before saying anything about Tarot, let us assume that you are a complete beginner who is just curious to know more and more about this enigmatic domain.

In very simple words, tarot is a deck of 78 cards which can be interpreted in different ways. People from various walks of life perceive its purpose in a whole new different way. For example, some claim that collective meditation on these cards creates an aura of energy around them. While some consider them to be a mode or channel of psychic phenomena, intuition, channel of communication with the spirits. In short, there are never ending theories and propositions about tarot cards.

One generic grounds, the cards are used for "psychic reading" or "tarot reading".

A Brief History

It should be noted that the origin of tarot cards remains a mystery. However, we do know that in 15th century – the Italians made use of these cards in a popular game card game. The wealthy people of the society commissioned beautiful decks. It is amazing to know that some of them have survived.

The eighteenth and nineteenth century marked the discovery of these cards by the influential scholars of occult. The cards fascinated these gentlemen and they came to the conclusion that the images on the cards were more than just a game. They had powerful meaning and idea behind them. This lead them to reveal (or create) the history of tarot. In this regard, they primarily connected the cards to the Hermetic philosophy, Egyptian mysteries, alchemy, the Kabbalah and other mystical systems. It should be noted that these pursuits were a major part of the 20th century and were incorporated in various societies.

The roots of the tarot lie in the occult tradition, however the interest started to increase only in the last few decades. Over the time, people have developed various perceptions and propositions about the tarot cards. In this regard, new cards have also been created. This is mainly due to the multifaceted interests of people belonging to different areas. There are different types in this regard. For example,

Native American

Dragon

Herbal

Japanese Deck

An interesting this to note is that tarot is commonly perceived as a tool for divination. The conventional mode of tarot reading involves two parties.

Seeker – Someone who wants answers to personal questions

Reader – Someone who has the knowledge of interpreting the cards

The seeker shuffles and cuts the deck. This step is followed by the laying out of the chosen cards. It should be noted that the cards are laid out in a specific pattern which is called spread. One of the interesting things to mention here is that each position of the spread holds a different meaning. Moreover, each card has a different meaning too. The reader concludes the final meaning based on the pattern of spread and meaning of each card. During the complete process, the reader is guided by the spiritual communication or psychic intuition.

At this point, you should note that it's not important to be psychic in order to read tarot successfully. On the other side of the picture, there is another proposition which states that you develop the qualities of psychic with training and practice. However, the case may differ based on the belief system of a person. You only need a little bit of intuition to read tarot cards effectively.

Chapter 6: Learning To Read Tarot Cards

You are going to have to spend some time with your cards if you want to learn how to read them correctly. There are many different types of decks available but I suggest that anyone who is first starting out purchase a pack of cards that has the meaning of the cards on the back of the deck. There are also decks that come with small booklets explaining the meaning of each card.

Because there are 78 cards in each deck I am not going to go into a lot of detail in this chapter about the meaning of each card but will give you a brief explanation. You can also use this as a quick reference when you are reading a spread.

Fool- New beginnings, innocence, starting something new or following a new path

Magician- Confidence, creating the life that you want, creation, represents the seeker if the seeker is male

The High Priestess- Mystery, secrets, if the seeker is female it may represent them if the seeker is male it can represent a female who is interested in the seeker.

The Empress- Represents fertility but can also represent a person who is materialistic. Can also represent safety, protection and satisfaction.

The Hierophant- Represents knowledge, usually based in traditional laws, rules or beliefs.

The Lover- Represents blessings, trust and harmony.

The Chariot- Represents strong emotion. Often it represents control in the situation, victory or victory by force.

Strength-Strong character, a person with courage or strong personal or spiritual convictions.

The Hermit- Usually associated with isolation but can also represent personal enlightenment or transformation.

The Wheel of Fortune- Represents change, foretells of destiny.

Justice- Represents fairness, the law as well as authority.

The Hanged Man- This card often means relinquishing what you have but depending on the situation it can also represent change. When the card is inverted can mean that the change is going to be negative but depending on where it is placed in the lay out it can mean that there are amazing changes coming into the seekers life as well.

Death- Many people automatically feel as if this is a bad card to draw but it actually represents a transition in the seekers life, this is something that is inevitable and must be accepted in order to progress to the next stage in life.

Temperance- Represents balance often the need of balance in the seekers life as well as moderation.

The Devil- This card represents corruption and ignorance. It can also mean that the seeker is resisting the changes that need to occur in their life.

The Tower- Represents the destruction of a foundation and cleansing the seeker. Depending on the situation it may be that the seeker needs to remove themselves from a specific relationship or even a job.

The Star- Represents a restoration of faith. Comfort.

The Moon- This card represents deception or an illusion what you perceive to be true is not what it seems.

The Sun- Success in whatever area the seeker is asking about, in a general reading the sun card represents success in life; celebration.

Judgment- This is another card that many people misinterpret but it represents rebirth, restoration and personal development.

The World- This card represents completion and achievements. This could be the completion of a goal or the completion of a relationship depending on where it is found in the spread.

Ace of Swords- This card represents power and clarity. It also represents achievement.

Two of Swords- This card usually means that the seeker is being defensive or stubborn when it comes to the situation they are seeking knowledge about. It can also mean that they are facing barriers in that specific situation.

Three of Swords- The seeker is facing a challenge in life, often faced with betrayal or is suffering from emotional pain.

Four of Swords- Most of the time this card means that the seeker need to rest or step away from a specific situation allowing their mind to recover from whatever has recently occurred.

Five of Swords- The seeker needs to open their eyes to the deception that is going on in their life.

Six of Swords- It is time to focus on balance in life, it is time for renewal.

Seven of Swords- Normally full of confidence the seeker is struggling with an important decision they need to make.

Eight of Swords- Although the seeker may feel as if they are helpless it is time for them to take control. They may feel as if they are lacking the courage and self-discipline to overcome a specific situation but they have the power within them.

Nine of Swords- The view of the world is distorted, the seeker is suffering from regret and anguish in their life.

Ten of Swords- Disaster is in the past and it is time for a rebirth, karma will give you what you deserve.

Page of Swords- The seeker has insight into the situation that they are not revealing to those around them.

Knight of Swords- Although the seeker may feel as if they are invincible and walk through life fearlessly they need to refrain from making sudden decisions at this time.

Queen of Swords- The seeker needs to follow their intuition about the specific situation, they have more wisdom than they admit and are able to see things clearly.

King of Swords- This card represents judgement. The seeker may be facing judgement, judging others or may be looking for an answer concerning a legal case. Either way the judgement is just.

Ace of Pentacles- The seeker has many resources that they may not even realize are there, they are blessed with many gifts and will reach their goals.

Two of Pentacles- The seeker needs to focus on balance in their life, they need to open themselves up to the changes that are coming, be flexible but also show restraint in their lives.

Three of Pentacles- The seeker needs to focus on cooperation if they want to see the fulfillment of their potential.

Four of Pentacles- This means that the person needs to look deep within themselves because they are suffering from greed and often they are hoarding something. They are only concerned about gaining and are very selfish. This could represent someone in the seekers life as well.

Five of Pentacles- This card represents misfortune, but not to worry there is always salvation.

Six of pentacles- This represents kindness and generosity but there needs to be discernment in the situation, don't allow others to take advantage of you.

Seven of Pentacles- Goals have been accomplished and it is time to reflect upon the choices you have made it is time for you to harvest.

Eight of Pentacles- Dedication is needed to get the experience desired.

Nine of Pentacles- You will have an abundance of satisfaction resulting in the building of your self-worth.

Ten of Pentacles- A possible inheritance is in the future this is time for sharing.

Page of Pentacles- A time to accept your responsibilities, grow your knowledge and take advantage of opportunities.

Knight of Pentacles- Success is coming your way but make sure you loyalties are where they should be.

Queen of Pentacles- Represents truthfulness, nurturing and generosity. This card can represent the seeker if they are female or a person that is interested in the seeker if they are a male.

King of Pentacles- Wealth is not out of reach, soon you will have the stability you have been looking for.

Chapter 7: Interpreting The Cards And Closing The Reading

Let us move on to the last two aspects of tarot reading session: interpreting the cards and then closing the reading.

Interpreting The Tarot Cards

Interpreting the cards isn't difficult at all. The first and most important thing you need to do is try to build a connection with a card and then try deciphering the message it wants to give you. You should also keep in mind the meanings of the Major Arcana cards you came across in the previous chapter and must consider them to interpret the tarot cards. In addition, you should keep in mind the following points to better comprehend their message.

• You need to notice the different colors in the card you draw out. Is it a colorful one, or can you mostly see just one color? Moreover, you need to focus on the meaning of that dominant color to you (if you're reading yourself), or the querent (if you're reading someone else.)

- You should also focus on the actions of the people illustrated on the cards. Are they communicating, standing, or struggling? What is it that they are doing and how does that make you feel?

- Moreover, you should also pay attention to the different symbols and elements appearing in your cards. What do they mean to you? If you see the devil reversed, then you need to focus on what does the devil mean to you? Your first step should be to concentrate on what an image or illustration means to you, and then bring into focus their original meanings.

In the start, you might not be able to quickly understand and interpret the meanings of the cards, but with routine practice, studying the tarot cards will become easy for you.

Closing The Tarot Reading

To close the tarot reading, you need to understand your inner feeling related to the reading. Do you feel it is time to close it? If yes, then hold the deck in both your hands. Next, pay your gratitude to the cards silently and thank them for guiding you today. Enjoy holding them close to you and keep expressing your thankfulness to them. This is a great exercise for improving your relationship with the cards. When your rapport with the cards strengthens, you are better able to connect to them and understand their guidance in a better manner. Once you are done thanking them, you need to put them aside.

Important Advice

To ensure you experience success in reading your tarot cards with time, you need to have in mind some important tips

- Practice regularly: You must read your cards frequently. The more you practice reading them, the better you'll get at this practice. However, you need to seek your intuition before beginning a reading. If you don't feel like reading the cards at a certain moment, then listen to your intuitive voice.

• Have Tarot Journal: Take a book and a pen, and label it 'My Tarot Journal.' You need to pen down all your stories and experiences related to your tarot readings in it. This will help you track your performance in reading the tarot from the time you started it. Moreover, you need to do a little exercise daily. Hold your deck and shuffle it. Then, divide it into half and draw a card from it. You can even put the cards with the image side facing you, and draw any card you like. Next, look at it closely and try to establish a feeling with it. How do you feel and what does the card mean to you? At this point, please ignore all the divinatory meanings and original symbolism of the card, and only focus on the card's imagery and the energy it is giving you. Describe that feeling in words and jot them down on your journal. If that illustration reminds you of a feeling, person, memory, dream or any emotion, please write it down. You must also write the name of the card you picked and the initial reaction and feeling you experienced on pulling it. This is a wonderful practice for connecting with the cards and truly understanding their meanings. As stated before, each card can hold a different meaning to different people, so don't worry about what an Emperor means to your friend or to any tarot expert, and focus mainly on what it tells you.

• Protect the cards: You must protect your cards from negative energies and physical damage. For that, you could wrap your cards in a soft scarf, preferably a silk one. This keeps your cards clean and safe from negative energies. You could also put them in a little box, or you could place them in a bag made from cloth and containing a drawstring, so you can pull the string to keep the cards safe. You can also ritually consecrate the cards, but it is a complicated procedure and best suited for advanced tarot readers. As a beginner, you should stick to the other protective methods discussed. You must never leave the cards scattered around the house because this exposes the cards to negative powers and increases their chances of many people touching them.

Chapter 8: Interpreting The Hidden Meanings Of Patterns(Including The Celtic Cross Spread)

A spread in tarot is a format, or the example where the peruser places the cards down on the table. Each position in the spread has an importance and adjusts the card set upon it. The Celtic Cross (CC) is the most broadly known and potentially the most generally utilized tarot spread. It is somewhat unpredictable for a flat out novice peruser, however it is well worth requiring some investment to learn and absorb it, as it might demonstrate to be the main spread you need, aside from the fundamental one, two and three-card readings.

The Celtic Cross was "imagined" by the well known medium, AE Waite, maker of the Rider-Waite tarot deck. So it is a genuinely present day gadget, albeit a few experts will have you accept something else! It is felt that he put together his renowned tarot spread with respect to a comparable one utilized in Europe, despite the fact that the birthplaces of that one are lost in the fogs of time.

I like to utilize a Celtic Cross as the "grapple" for my readings for customers. It is perfect for explaining circumstances and bringing out extra questions. It's critical to not utilize it aimlessly, for instance, if perusing for yourself, it is totally futile doing a full-length CC perusing consistently. It bodes well to confine its utilization to once per month, or even less often. I have found over my numerous long stretches of tarot perusing that the data offered by a decent, inside and out Celtic Cross can keep on unfurling more than a year or more.

Prior to Laying Out the Cards

You presumably have your very own strategy for directing your readings, and that is great. Notwithstanding, one thing I prescribe before starting is to disclose to the customer that this format is perfect for connection. I reveal to them I'm an instinctive peruser, not a clairvoyant or a scoundrel who is searching for "signs", and that they will get more from the perusing on the off chance that they take an interest. This breaks the ice and comforts us both. There is nothing more terrible than attempting to peruse for somebody who creases their arms in dread of "parting with something". I like my readings to be a two-way process.

Cards One and Two: The Heart of the CC

Position One: The Current Situation or Challenge

The primary card outlines the fundamental circumstance that faces the searcher. It tends to be something they know about, or perhaps something they are careless in regards to yet will make its quality known really soon. In the event that you can't quickly pinpoint the test, quickly utilize the card significance to depict the kind of circumstance that card many speak to and inquire as to whether it implies anything to them. Ordinarily, the conditions become more clear as you progress through the perusing.

In our model, above, we see that the searcher is being tested by a circumstance spoke to by the Five of Swords. Fives are consistently difficulties in themselves, and this one inclines toward scholarly or correspondence issues. Here, we see that there is some contest going on, or perhaps the searcher is associated with a harassing effort.

Position Two: Obstacles and Blocks

The second for the most part shows the deterrents or squares to the goals of the issue, and remember that there is commonly an "issue" or the customer wouldn't need a perusing in any case. Frequently, this card speaks to someone else or someone else's desires.

For you, the peruser, it is imperative to peruse these cards as a couple; nearly as one card, on the off chance that you like. Take a gander at the pictures. Do they help or restrict? Is there a story there? Do they help you to remember anything in your own life? Stand up, say what you see—making sure to be prudent and aware of your customer's sensibilities, obviously.

As should be obvious, these two cards can quickly explain the circumstance, consequently the possibility this, occasionally, is all the individual needs. They can envision their conditions, as though from a goal stance. It merits asking them, what guidance they would offer to somebody in a similar circumstance. The "aha!" minutes that question incites are extremely valuable.

In the model, the searcher is looked with the Five of Cups—an enthusiastic test this time. This demonstrates whatever is appeared in card one, has brought about a misfortune or profound lament, and that it is this which is keeping the searcher from moving past the issue.

Positions Three to Six

Card Three is the base or foundation of the present circumstance. It can speak to impacts from the quick past right back to youth. I by and large look to this card as the purpose behind the perusing.

Card Four is what is previously or is in the present, yet previously subsiding. On the off chance that there are negative cards in the perusing, this is the place I would want to see them.

Card Five represents what the customer is moving towards, or what the customer sees as a result. I have heard this position called the "expectations and fears" or "elective result" card. As it were, it shows the "Law of Attraction" in real life. Frequently what the querent accepts will happen *will* occur. It is helpful to peruse this as a couple with Card 10.

Card Six is what is in the quick future or is now moving into the present. Take a gander at cards four, one, two and six. They speak to a course of events. Take as much time as is needed to reevaluate them and attempt to get the string of the story.

Cards Seven to Ten

Card Seven is significant. It shows what impacts the querent brings to the circumstance. It can speak to their feelings, activities and suppositions. See this card with the card in the third position, and you will show signs of improvement picture of where the customer is coming from. The two cards, together, will frequently reveal to you more than the customer is letting on.

Card Eight. The card in this position speaks to other individuals in the circumstance. Their impact, sentiments and feelings. It could likewise speak to a gathering or an establishment. At the end of the day, it is "the other". Take a gander at this with Card 7—check whether there is a "pushing against" going on. Two restricting powers, neither ready to surrender their position. Remember this can likewise be a helping position—the card may show somebody who can help.

Card Nine is frequently viewed as direction or an option "expectations and fears". I like to consider it the trump card... furthermore, don't dole out it a significance until I see what card turns up here. It tends to be the vital card and offer the response to the issue.

Card Ten is the result if everything remains the equivalent. At the end of the day, if the querent proceeds with the way without rolling out an improvement. You can peruse this as a couple with Card Five; they will regularly depict the future with incredible precision.

Time-Line Tip

Once you have dealt with the cards in their logical order, you can read pairs and combinations where appropriate; shift your attention to the time-line indicated by cards four, one, two and six, as mentioned above. This can be quite revealing as you have a nice, pure little past, present, future spread right there. Card three is the recent past, one and two are the present and current situation, and card six is the near future.

These cards can also be interpreted in an energetic way rather than as a fortune-telling manner. In this case, you would look at influences and energies that the seeker is leaving behind; influences and energies they are dealing with in the present and influences and energies moving toward them.

Celtic Cross Tips

A few perusers like to bargain the cards face down and turn them more than individually. I discover it undeniably progressively valuable to just flip the cards down, face-up. I like to pause for a moment to retain the general kind of the spread. You can get a quick feel regarding whether the perusing will be "up" or "down". In the two cases, you should ensure that the perusing and exhortation given leaves the customer feeling inspired, or if nothing else progressively positive. I like to utilize the perusing to get my customer to take control, and the cards are incredible at indicating where they are allowing things to occur and where they can start to make changes.

Disclose to the customer that the perusing focuses towards activities, occasions and circumstances that could unfurl more than a while. Offer them the opportunity to hit you up with respect to this perusing. It will help you colossally in the event that you set aside the effort to note down the cards. Later you can include a short abstract of the perusing you gave, significant focuses that the customer brought up and any issues emerging.

Ordinarily, a Celtic Cross takes some at any rate 45 minutes to experience. The rest of the time is offered over to a couple of short readings to address addresses that the customer may have.

Chapter 9: The Study Of Minor Arcana

The Tarot is made out of 78 cards, 56 cards called the minor arcana and 22 cards called the major arcana. The 56 minor arcana are framed of 4 arrangement of 14 cards each. The 22 significant arcana are shaped of 21 numbered cards and of 1 un-numbered.

We will come back to the cause of this superb origination of the human personality, yet for the present, we should bind ourselves to the dismemberment of the machine, and the presentation of its puzzling course of action. Beginning from a fixed and unflinching guideline, the constitution of the Sacred Tetragrammaton' Yod-he-vau-he, the Tarot builds up the most different mixes, without one takeoff from its premise.

We will currently disclose this superb development, which affirms in its application the all-inclusive law of analogies. The clarifications which pursue may seem dry to certain people, yet they should recall that we are here giving them a practically trustworthy key to the old or mysterious science, and they will comprehend that they should open the entryway of the sacred curve for themselves.

STUDY OF A SUIT

Give us now a chance to take one of the bundles of fourteen cards and break down its development. This parcel, taken all in all, relates to one of the suits of our pack of cards. The 4 parcels separately speak to the Wands or Scepters, relating to our clubs; the Cups or Goblets, comparing to our souls; the Swords, relating to our spades; and Money or Pentacles, comparing to our precious stones. We will currently contemplate one of these parcels, for example, that of Scepters. The bundle comprises of 4 figures: the ruler, sovereign, knight and miscreant, and of ten cards which just bear numbers, the ace, two, three, four, five, six, seven, eight, nine and ten.

THE FOUR PICTURES

We should initially consider the court cards. The ruler speaks to the dynamic, the man, or the male. The sovereign speaks to the latent, the lady, or the female. The knight speaks to the fix, the juvenile. Ultimately, the villain speaks to the fourth term of the grouping, which might be figured along these lines, King, Queen, Knight, and Knave. This grouping is just a use of the general law YOD-HE-VAU-he, which we definitely know, and the similarity is effectively settled.

The miscreant, in this manner, relates to the subsequent "He" for example, it is just a term of change. However, progress between what? Between the four figures and the ten numbers following.

THE TEN NUMBERS

Let us next investigate these numbers. We are familiar with the Law of numbers, or the law of the arrangements, which we have just expressed in these terms. The ten cards can't escape from this law, and we may without a moment's delay orchestrate them in an arrangement. The main arrangement will be framed of the expert, or 1, speaking to the dynamic; of the 2, personating the detached; of the 3 for the fix; and finally of the 4, which speaks to the progress starting with one arrangement then onto the next. 1, 2, 3, 4, in this manner, relate additionally with the YOD-HE-VAU-HE and are in this way figured.

The different arrangement keep a similar standard precisely, the second He of the previous arrangement turning into the YOD of the accompanying arrangement: therefore 4, the fourth term of the principal arrangement, he comes to the main term of the subsequent arrangement; we see that a similar law, YOD-HE-VAU-HE, can be applied to these arrangements. Since this law is likewise relevant to the four figures, we can make a correlation dependent on 011 the accompanying recommendation.

Two terns (the numbers and the figures) equivalent to a similar third (the law YOD-HE-VAU-HE) are equivalent between themselves. Figure 10, in this manner, represents the numbers as the villain represents the figures, in other words, it fills in as a change. Between what? Between one suit and another.

AFFINITY BETWEEN THE PICTURES AND THE NUMBERS

We have just concentrated both the photos and the numbers independently; let us currently observe what association exists between them. On the off chance that we bunch comparable terms as indicated by the indistinguishable Law which rules them, we will discover them as pursues.

The King is the Yod of 1. 4. 7

The Queen — He of 2. 5. 8

The Knight — Vau of 3. 6. 9

The Knave — second He of 10

The arrangement of the photos is repeated multiple times in the arrangement of numbers, in other words, every arrangement of numbers speaks to the origination of the photos in every one of the three Kabalistic universes.

The arrangement 1, 2, 3, 4 speaks to the radiation of the grouping lord, sovereign, kinglet, villain, in the divine world. Arrangement 4, 5, 6, 7 speaks to this development in the human world. The arrangement 7, 8, 9, 10 speaks to this development in the material world. Every one of these parts can subdivide itself into three others, as the numbers demonstrate. 1 Let us, be that as it may, come back to our reasoning, and by summarizing the outcomes, we will discover Representations of the Yod:

STUDY OF THE FOUR SUITS

Provided with this information, let us proceed with our investigation and apply a similar rule to different cards. The laws which we have characterized for the constitution of one suit, apply similarly to the next three suits. In any case, when we think about the four suits of the Tarot, new findings will be called forward. We should recollect that these suits are: the Scepter, the Cup, the Sword, and the Money or Pentacles. The Scepter speaks to the Male or the Active.

The Cup is the picture of the Passive or Feminine. The Sword speaks to the association of the two by its essential structure. Ultimately, the Pentacles speak to the subsequent "He". The creators who have thoughtfully contemplated the Tarot are on the whole consistent in stating the similarity that exists between the Tetragrammaton, and the four suits. William Postel 1 or more all Eliphas Levi 2 have built up these investigations with significant outcomes, and they show us the four letters of Tetragrammaton, applied in the imagery of each clique.

We should delay one minute to see the relationship between these letters and the images of the Christian religion. The Yod or Scepter of the Tarot is spoken to by the episcopal crosier. The first He or Cup is spoken to by the Chalice; the Vau or Sword by the Cross, bearing a similar structure. The second He or Pentacles by the Host, the change from the common to the Supernatural world.

The arrangement which we have considered in one suit is characterized with equivalent severity in the four suits viewed all in all, in this way.

A COMPREHENSIVE GLANCE AT THE MINOR ARCANA

On the off chance that we think back a bit, we can without much of a stretch judge the street so far navigated. The four suits considered in globs have indicated to us the utilization of the law Yod-he-vau-he. Be that as it may, a similar law is recreated in every one of the suits taken independently. The four court cards speak to Yod-he-van-he; the four arrangement of numbers speaks to the Sacred Name in like way.

Engineered outline, we cover to place the Sacred Name in the focal point of a hover partitioned into four sections, which individuals relate with right on time of the letters Yod-he-vau-he. In every one of the quarters, the cards that are practically equivalent to the letters of Tetragrammaton will emanate from the inside. See the outline on the page inverse. The photos have an indistinguishable association with the suits from the numbers have with the photos. The succession of the photos is replicated in the three universes by the numbers; something very similar happens in the arrangement of suits: Scepter, Cup, Sword, Pentacles are duplicated in the photos.

It is conceivable just to demonstrate the informative affinities that appeared in these figures; they can be created at incredible length. We give the exposed layouts to show the strategy for similarity, the technique for mysterious science, to which we have so as often as possible suggested our previous works. We need just think about this last graph, which speaks to the four suits, with the primary, which portrayed one of them just, to see immediately that the law whereupon the two outlines are built is the equivalent, however, its applications are changed.

It is a similar law by which the cells that structure the person bunch themselves to establish organs; the organs bunch themselves to frame individuals; and the gathering of the last creates the person. We may reach the accompanying inference from distress that we have just expressed that The Pentacles, reacting to the subsequent He, show a change. Between what? Between the minor and major arcana.

Chapter 10: Pentacles

The Pentacles depict practicality and material concerns. They indicate that you enjoy interactions with nature and celebrate every little joy.

Ace of pentacles- the upright ace of pentacles indicates that you are going to have new beginnings in your life. Like most other aces, it indicates that you are going to have fresh starts and go into something with a lot of energy and enthusiasm. It also signifies wealth and that you are going to have a lot of income doling in. it also signifies abundance and it need not always be mere financial abundance. You will have a lot of love and good energy surrounding you. You will also have lots of material things that will help make your life wonderful. This card showcases a beautiful garden with plants and a hand emerging from a cloud and supporting the sun with a pentacle inside it. You can instantly feel the positivity that this card brings with it. The reversed ace of pentacles card signifies that you are not prepared to identify your opportunities and have let them slip through your hands. You have not capitalized on taking up a good job offer or said yes to a rise in your pay. You do not have clear thinking and no plans for your future.

Two of pentacles- the upright two of pentacles card indicates that you a clear conscious and know exactly how to balance the different aspects of your life. You know how to manage your work and also know how to balance your family life. You do not let the two aspects mix together and have everything planned and sorted out. You juggle your finances, family and health and are in a great position to manage all with equal control. The card showcases a young man dancing and holding two pentacles each in both his hands. There is an infinity loop around them, which suggests that the man is capable of tackling an infinite number of problems. The man looks slightly concerned but nothing that stops him from dancing. The reversed two of pentacles card signifies that you are not at all organized and there is a lot of imbalance in your personal and professional life. It means that you are not keeping up with your professional and personal commitments and are running away from responsibility. You are not planning your expenses and incomes and ending up wasting them. If you are in a new relationship then it is best to not go overboard with your promises and try and keep it as reasonable as possible without getting carried away.

Three of pentacles- the upright three of pentacles card indicates that you are doing well in life and are achieving whatever you set out to achieve. You are good at planning and fulfilling your material goals and the arrival of this card indicates that you need to keep up with the good work. It is a card to encourage you and get you to work harder. You need to remain inspired and turn to others for your inspiration. The card showcases a young mason who is sculpting something on the cathedral's wall. He has sculpted three beautiful pentacles. He is speaking with two others who appear to be his guides. They seem to be listening to what he has to say. The young man is also open to seek advice from the two older monks. The reversed three of pentacles signify that you are not organized and are relying too much on others. If your group is not working well then you are not going to make positive progress. It will also indicate that you are not being recognized enough at your work place and are looking to be respected more. You should also break free and remain independent.

Four of pentacles- the upright four of pentacles card signifies that you are extremely successful and have achieved a lot of things in life. These include material things such as money, wealth and overall success. This is a great thing no doubt but on the flipside, you have turned extremely greedy and are not satisfied with what you have. You want more and more and are blinded by your greed. The card showcases a young man who is sitting on a stool placed away from his town. He has a pentacle on his head and one in his hand. He is stamping a couple of pentacles below his feet. This signifies that he is under so much pressure to hold on to these that he cannot even move. He has a smile to indicate that he is happy. The reversed four of pentacles indicate that the person is not in a position to trust anyone, as you fear they will take away your material possessions. This means that you are constantly hounded by worry of losing your possessions and are holding on to them as tightly as possible. If this card comes by then it indicates that you need to loosen your grip a bit and try and trust others.

Five of pentacles- the upright five of pentacles card implies that you are stuck financially and are losing your money. You might also be poor and are not able to amass any money. You are suffering from ne failure after another and it is causing you to worry in excess. You have allowed emotions to guide you that have caused your downfall. The arrival of this card indicates that you showcased a lot of pride in your wealth and it has been taken away from you for being so proud. The card showcases a cripple and an old lady walking past a window that has five pentacles drawn on it. The reversed five of pentacles card indicates that you are now recovering from a financial loss and are in a good position to become self-sufficient again. You have found yourself a benefactor who wishes to help you through your tough times. It is also an indication of you having lost touch with your spiritual side and how that is causing you to become extremely materialistic. You need to turn spiritual again if you wish to find material success in life.

Six of pentacles- the upright six of pentacles card signifies that you are extremely generous and don't think twice before helping people in need. You believe in charity and giving to others. And the more you give away, the more you get back. You have already amassed quite a lot and are in a position to help as many people as possible. You will also give away loans to those in need and almost always have them repay you. The card showcases a well-dressed man standing between two beggars and holding a balance in one hand. He is dropping gold coins from the other hand and the beggars have a relived and thankful expression on their face. There are six pentacles drawn above the man. If you are the beggars that are signifies on the card then you are soon going to find the benefactor who will give you money. The reversed six of pentacles card signifies that you are giving away loans and money but are not making it back. People are taking you for granted and literally cheating you. They are running away with your money. It might also show that you are only giving money because you are trying to prove to others how whole hearted you are and not giving it because you want to help others.

Seven of pentacles- the upright seven of pentacles card indicates that you wish to make timely and profitable investments that will help you benefit in the long run. You are not keen on witnessing short-term gains and wish to have your money bear fruit in the long run. You are capable of putting in the right efforts to see positive growth. The card showcases a young man who is resting his chin on a spade. He stands next to a plant that has pentacles for fruits and one is on the ground. He is gazing at the plant and is taking pride in what he has successfully grown. The reversed seven of pentacles card indicates that you doubt whether your investments will give you positive results. It says that you are suddenly overcome by doubt and yet, continue to toil. In terms of relationships, you are trying your best to invest in a long-term relationship but are unable to establish one.

Eight of pentacles- the upright eight of pentacles indicates that you are interested in learning and taking up internships. You are ready to put in a lot of hard work and fulfill your desires. You are up for learning anything. The card shows a young man carving out pentacles on eight coins. He has finished 5, is working on the sixth and has two more to go. He is paying keen attention to it and not distracted by anything. The reversed eight of pentacles can indicate that the person is not ambitious enough and is bothered by the world. You have just one focus and don't consider other things. If you are slightly disturbed then you will lose your concentration and end up doing a shoddy job. You might also leave your job incomplete.

Nine of pentacles- the upright nine of pentacles card indicates that you are financially happy and self-sufficient. You have amassed success and wealth and are now living in the lap of luxury. You are now reaping the fruits of your hard work and living an amazing life. The card showcases a mature woman walking in a plush garden and is surrounded by grape wines. She is wearing a golden robe and is surrounded by nine pentacles. She is holding a bird in her hand and gazing lovingly at it. The reversed nine of pentacles can signify financial losses. It will also indicate that you are spending too much time working and compromising on a personal life. Although you have amassed quite a bit, you are not enjoying it. There are several blocks that are causing you to not be satisfied or are constantly trying to attain more from life.

Ten of pentacles-the upright ten of pentacles indicates that you are on the verge of completing something and in for a stroke of gold luck. You are either about to retire and have a good life or come into inherited fortune. You are going to have a good family life and your will come into great power and wealth. The card showcases an old man sitting outside his house and I surrounded by plush grape wines. He is also surrounded by his dogs and grand children and is overlooking his happy family. There are pentacles strewn all over the card. The reversed ten of pentacles showcases the blockage in this kind of a happy picture. There is something stopping you from having it. You have family fights and are not able to enjoy your wealth. You are also not able to access your grandchildren or other close relatives and it is causing you worry.

Page of pentacles- the upright page of pentacles indicates a new job or a new opportunity for you to increase your financial position. You have a lot of good ideas and it is the best time for you to put them into action. The card showcases a young man standing in the middle of a garden and holding a pentacle up high. He has a curious look on his face, which indicates that he is interested in maximizing his gains. The reversed page of pentacles indicates that there are a few blocks in you trying to attain your dream job or making money. You will have to spend time in reevaluating your resources and use them wisely to help you improve your opportunity grabbing skills. It will also indicate that you are not looking at the bigger picture and are only interested in something of a short-term nature. It is time for you to look into long lasting gains.

Knight of pentacles- the upright knight of pentacles card indicates that you are extremely organized and methodic and a visionary. You are a responsible person and do not shy away from commitment. You are trustworthy and capable of providing to all those that are dependent on you. In fact, you are a perfectionist and looked up to by many around you. You put your mind to something and don't stop until you have achieved it. This card can be an indication for you to continue doing what you are and not stop it. The card showcases a young knight sitting on a horse and holding a pentacle in his hand. He looks determined and in a good position to fulfill all his goals. The reversed knight of pentacles card indicates that the person is easily bored and is also quite restless. You often forgo the upkeep of important things in your mundane life and prefer to concentrate on something that has caught your fancy. You might not be adventurous enough and prefer to remain in your comfort zone.

Queen of pentacles- the upright queen of pentacles card indicates that you are homely and a reliable person. You are down to earth and believe in pleasing others. You genuinely care for them and cook for them, clean for them and do things that will make others happy. You need not always be a mother yourself and can also be a mother figure. You can be a counselor and someone that others come to for advice for all the main decisions of life. Basically you will take on the role of someone who is looked up to and also considered to be a lucky mascot. People will regard you as being a compassionate and loving person who always has something to give to others. The card showcases a queen sitting on her throne in the middle of a forest. She holds a big pentacle in her hand and is looking down lovingly. There is a rabbit that is running which implies fertility. The reversed queen of pentacles card can indicate that you are feeling isolated and homebound. You are feeling trapped and unable to move forward. You seek financial independence but don't have the means for it. It might also mean that you are becoming over caring and although you really do care for these people your love is smothering them and making them repulsive. You might hurt because of it and need to reevaluate who to love and who not to. You can also take a back seat and allow people to miss your love, as that is the only way they will realize how precious you are.

King of pentacles- the upright king of pentacles card indicates having a lot of security and power. You are extremely disciplined and trustworthy. You are the father figure that most people look up to. You are a great provider and provide several people with wealth and daily needs. You personify financial stability and set an example to others. You are one of those that anyone will trust and be ready to tie up with. This is because they will be confident in your approach to business and trust your judgment in making good profits. You are also extremely alert and in a good position to take major decisions within a short time's notice. You are a loving and caring partner and your partner will be extremely happy with you. The card showcases the king sitting on a heavily decorated throne and is surrounded by vines full of grapes. He wields a scepter in his hand and has a pentacle in his other hand. The reversed king of pentacles indicates being stubborn and not having an open mindset. The person will be old fashioned and expect others to behave in a traditional way. The arrival of this reversed card can indicate that you are making friends only for their wealth and the same extends to lovers. Once you exploit them financially you will discard them and move to another. You might also physically abuse them to try and exploit their money.

These conclude all the minor arcana cards and hope you have understood what each one stands for.

Chapter 11: Tarot Spells And Rituals
Basic Tarot Spells

There is one more thing that you need to be aware of before starting your practice, because it can play an essential part in the act of reading: your personal state of mind and the temporal and spatial conditions.

The truth is that, if you want, you can use your tarot cards in any place and in any moment of the day, but if something else distracts you (be it a personal worry or a powerful noise from the outside), you won't be able to stay focused, and concentrate only on the specific question that you are trying to answer. This is why it's recommended (not essential) to create an environment favorable to the action that is to be performed.

Put simply, a ritual is a specific series of behaviors and practices that are enacted sequentially for social, religious, spiritual, emotional or ceremonial purposes. Rituals are commonly associated with landmark moments – births, deaths, marriages – and they can bring joy, ease sorrow, or just celebrate something major. Rituals are in essence repetitive – like a routine. The same order is observed every time the ceremony is performed, and many people find security in that familiarity.

The point here is that there are many, many different ways to perform tarot rituals, depending on the personal preferences of the participants, the purpose of the ritual, the location, and numerous other factors.

It's no exaggeration to say there are probably millions of permutations for performing tarot rituals. However, there is a sequence of events that need to be observed if you are to obtain everything you require from your rituals, and this is what is meant when referring to the 'correct' way. If you haven't already noticed, when it comes to rituals, tarot is both a personal and universal religion.

The word 'ritual' does not suggest spontaneity. A ritual consists of individual elements, performed in a particular sequence. Whenever the ritual is repeated, the elements and sequence will also be repeated. tarot rituals are also like that – they are designed with a purpose, and in order to make the ritual work as you want it to, you need to prepare thoroughly. That means preparing yourself, the items you will use during the ritual, the area where it will be conducted, and the words that will be spoken during.

You may wish to consider what – if any – clothing you will wear for a particular ritual. Does it require a ritual bath, or just regular bodily cleansing, which should be part of the ritual preparation anyway? All these things need to be considered during the preparation for the ritual.

This preparation serves several purposes, and it is crucial to the success of the ritual. Preparation concentrates the mind on what will take place during the ritual, and what you are seeking to gain from it. And if your preparations are thorough, you can relax and enjoy the ritual, because it is something to be enjoyed, rather than endured.

How to perform tarot rituals?

You need to take care of a few things before practicing a reading, during the reading and then after you have conducted it. This helps you make the most of a reading and benefit from it. Here is what you need to do:

Things You Must Do Before a Tarot Reading

If you observe the following tips and practices prior to conducting a tarot reading, you will be able to perform it with a positive frame of mind and extract great lessons from it.

Meditate

Meditation is a great way to attain peace of body and mind that can help you stay focused during the practice. While you should meditate on a regular basis, it is wise to meditate for 5 to 10 minutes 30 to 60 minutes prior to conducting a tarot session.

While there are many ways to meditate, here is a simple breathing meditative technique for you that requires you to use your breath as the object of your focus. Here is how you can carry it out.

Sit somewhere quiet and peaceful, and think of a relaxing memory. You can also play some soothing music in the background to relax your stressed nerves.

When you feel calmer, close your eyes and very gently and slowly, bring your attention to your breath.

You need to inhale at your own pace, but through your nose and exhale through your mouth.

Every time you do that, make sure to watch your breath and observe how it moves from the outside environment inside your body, circulates inside it and then exits it through your mouth.

Keep doing that for a good 5 to 10 minutes and every time you wander off in thought, just gently bring your attention back to your thoughts.

Open your eyes when you end your session and enjoy the nice, peaceful feeling you have created inside you.

You are likely to feel quite relaxed than before. Now is the time to think about your questions and then carry out the tarot reading session. You can also meditate before exploring the answers of a reading or reflecting on it again so you do it with a clear, cleansed mind.

Prepare All Your Questions Beforehand

You must identify your goal for conducting a tarot reading beforehand so when you have it, you are clear and focused on what you want. For that, it is best to prepare your questions beforehand preferably after you are done meditating.

You are likely to feel more relaxed and focused after your meditation session, and are likely to think more clearly so that would be a good time to think about the questions you would like to explore in the reading.

Prepare a list of questions regarding a specific issue or goal you wish to accomplish from having a particular reading. When you carry out the reading, you need to focus on those questions, one at a time.

Visualize the Preferred Outcome

Specific tarot experts advise the querents to think about the preferred outcome or answer prior to having a tarot reading. This goes back to employing the power of positive affirmation to rewire your subconscious mind to think about a specific outcome so you become motivated to achieve it.

Therefore, if you would like to achieve financial independence and overcome the economic crisis you are going through currently, think about how you have managed to resolve your financial problems and are moving towards a period of great wealth and abundance.

This in any way does not imply that you will change the outcome of your tarot card reading or make the cards show you what you want from within. It just means you prepare your mind to think positively so even if the cards show something complete opposite, you accept it with an optimistic mindset and are ready to extract good things from it and achieve what you truly want.

If you work on these tips, you are likely to have a tarot reading with complete clarity and get something good out of it.

Things to Do During the Reading

During the reading, you need to take care of a few important things to ensure you stay on the right track.

Brush Up Your Knowledge of the Cards

Before conducting the reading, brush up your knowledge of all the major arcana cards especially if you intend to focus on an important, life-altering episode you have faced or are going through. You should know each of the major arcana cards meanings and the elements they are related to. You must also be aware of the meanings and associations of minor arcana cards, and how they can influence you. While you can refer to the meanings in between a reading, it is still wiser to have a better know-how of them beforehand.

Think of the Bigger Picture/ Question in Focus

Think of the bigger picture and then the problem at hand before pulling out the cards so you know what you have to focus on.

Pay Attention to Different Elements

When reading the cards, do not just focus on the main message or meaning of a card, but also pay attention to the little details on them including the imagery, symbols, signs, colors, expressions of the characters on the cards, actions of the images and characters and what each character, symbol and expression means to you. If you see an angel on the card, what does that mean to you and how do you perceive it.

Be Patient

During the reading, be patient with yourself, your thoughts and the cards. If you see a card that does not make you feel happy, do not hold on to that feeling and instead, continue with the reading with a positive attitude because you do not know what the next card may have in store for you.

Study with an Unbiased Attitude

You need to keep your attitude as objective and unbiased as possible throughout the reading. Do not hold judgments related to individual cards or characters on them, and do not wish for only certain cards to show. Instead, keep a very positive and neutral state of mind, and wish to unlock the truth and wisdom associated with your problems.

Things to Take Care of After the Reading

Here are some things you need to implement after a tarot reading to become better at the practice:

Close the Reading on a Positive Note

Whatever you learned from the reading, close it on a positive note by thanking the cards for the lessons they taught you and building the determination to change your life for the better.

Cleanse and Clean Your Cards

Your cards pick up energies from you and from the outside environment, and these energies can interfere with your tarot reading and can influence the results you see. To ensure you get the most out of every reading, you need to cleanse your cards on a regular basis. You can do that in several ways. First, you need to put your cards in a clean, silk pouch in a clean box in a de-cluttered room. Secondly, you can place your cards open in a window on a full moon night. Moonlight is very cleansing and will beautifully cleanse your cards of all the negativity they have picked on overtime. You can also put some sweet grass or white sage incense in a room where you put your tarot cards.

The scent of the incense is cleansing and will purify your cards of any toxicity it has picked up from the environment or from anyone who has used or picked those cards.

Keep the Cards Safe

You need to ensure the cards are kept in good condition and ensure that not too many people pick and use them. You should be the one or one of the 2 to 3 people using the cards to make them familiar with your touch and presence.

Also, if too many people use the cards, they will absorb a plethora of energies and become infected.

Practice

Practice tarot reading at least once every week to slowly get the hang of it and get better at interpreting the cards.

Esoteric Tarot divination

Many believe that this is guided by spiritual energy whilst there are those who think that the cards, in fact, help them in tapping into a collective unconscious. Of course, the mere mention of the occult can scary most of the people. In fact, this is exactly what happened during a period in the tarot's use. While it was first meant for entertainment and gaming, its popularity really peaked when its use for divination became more widespread.

In fact, it was considered to be the Devil's picture book (and perhaps, many people still consider it as such) and was referred to as the work of evil by one Dominican preacher who gave a fiery sermon about the cards and its malice.

The idea of these cards being a mystical key was furthered by Eliphas Levi. This man received his education in the seminary of Saint-Sulipice and was also ordained deacon but never went on to become a priest. It is said that notes from Levi's book called "Dogme et rituel" form the foundation for the modern-day occultist movement. In this book, Levi claims to have discovered a secret of great value but was hidden in ancient parables as well as esoteric obfuscation.

This secret would be that there is a Lux (astral light or light) that flows behind everything and is also contained within every corner of reality itself. When it comes to the tarot, he claims to be the first person to discover an unknown yet intact key to all philosophies and doctrines in the ancient world. "Without the tarot, the Magic of the Ancients is a closed book."

Chapter 12: Tarot Spreads

Tarot spreads are the way we lay out the cards to do readings. Each spread is for a different purpose. The spread can be a simple three card spread to go over your past, present, and future. Or it can be as complicated as having twenty cards, and include your feelings, rivalries, disputes, and other outside factors. Reading a tarot spread is like reading a story. The important part to remember in all of this is that the result is not permanent. You have the ability to choose your own fate. Since the cards are giving you only one outcome you can make the choice to do something else and have a different outcome from the one provided. Just remember your choices have consequences as well and if you change something your outcome does change whether it is for the better or worse is for you to find out.
Three Card Spread

This is the simplest spread. You shuffle your cards thinking of your question the entire time. You will pick three cards that will tell the past, present, and future of your query. This is a good spread to start with doing yourself daily. If you are doing this spread with another person they will be the person shuffling the cards and thinking about what they want to know. They will also be picking the three cards out of the deck. Another way of looking at this spread is where you stand now with a present difficulty, how you can get what you want, and what may stop you or help you get it.

The Celtic Cross

This is a very common spread used widely to answer a specific question the person has. There are 10 cards. The first cards is laid down, the second card is laid down cross ways on top of it. The third card is laid below the first card. The fourth card is laid to the left of the first card. The fifth

card is laid above the first card. The sixth card is laid to the right of the first card. Then cards seven, eight, nine and ten are laid to the right of the sixth card in a line up from the seventh card to the tenth card at the top. Everything can be laid with the cards facing down so you can turn the cards over one by one or the cards laid right side up at the time that you pick them, just make sure that when you lay down the cards you are paying attention to whether the cards are upright or reversed, since they will have different meanings depending upon which way they are laying.
Also each cards stands for a particular part of the question. The first card is what controls the questioner? The second card is what obstructions are around the questioner? The third question is how did the current position come into being? The fourth card is about the distant past the questioner has had to deal with regarding the problem. The fifth card is what goal does the questioner what to reach? The sixth card is what does the future hold for

the questioner about the problem? The seventh card is what is the questioner's outlook on the problem? The eighth card is how do others see the questioner? The ninth card is the questioner's dreams and what scares them about the problem. And the tenth card is the conclusion and what will happen to the questioner regarding the problem.

Are They the One?

The first card is laid out in the middle of the top row. The second card is laid below the first card on the second row. The third card is laid to the left of the first card in the first row. The fourth card is laid to the right of the first card on the first row. The fifth card is laid below the third card on the third row. The sixth card is laid below the fourth card on the third row. The seventh card is laid below the second card on the third row. The first card represents whether the person is the one. The second card represents if there will be an engagement or other obligation to each other in the future. The third card represents anything negative about the relationship. The fourth card represents all things positive about the relationship. The fifth card represents what the questioner can do to be ready for their love to enter into their life. The sixth card represents what the other person needs to do to become a part of the questioner's life. The seventh card represents will they be happy together?

Tree of Life

This spread looks at all aspects of a person's life and tries to find the obstructions to get around and assistance that will help them make their life better.

The first card is laid at the top. The second card is laid to the right on the second row. The third card is laid to the left on the second row. The fourth card is laid under the second card on the third row. The fifth card is laid under the third card on the third row. The sixth card is laid under the first card on the fourth row. The seventh card is laid under the fourth card on the fifth row. The eighth card is laid under the fifth card on the fifth row. The ninth card is laid under the sixth card in the sixth row. The tenth card is laid under the ninth card on the seventh row. The first card represents spiritual occurrence. The second card represents obligations. The third card represents questions we must answer and trials we must go through. The fourth card represents helpful circumstances. The fifth card represents Conflicting, circumstances. The sixth card represents accomplishments. The seventh card represents impassioned relationships. The eighth card represents messages and jobs. The ninth card represents your support. And the tenth card represents your house and kin. Which Job Should I Get?

This spread looks like a big triangle. And many people these days have problems choosing jobs, especially ones that follow their passion.

The first card is the top of the triangle. The second card is on the second row down and to the left. The third card is on the second row, down and to the right. The fourth card is on the third row down and to the left. The fifth card is on the fourth row down and to the left, the left triangle point. The sixth card is on the fourth to the right of the fifth card. The seventh card is on the third row down and on the right of the third card. The eighth card is on the fourth row to the right of the sixth card. And the ninth card is on the fourth row to the right of the eighth card and the right triangle point. The first card represents what the questioner is wanting in a job. The second card represents what the questioner likes about the first job. The third card represents what the questioner likes about the second job. The fourth card represents appeal of the first job. The fifth card represents the advantages of the first job. The sixth card represents the bad things about the first job. The seventh card represents the appeal of the second

job. The eighth card represents the advantages of the second job. And the ninth card represents the bad things about the second job.
Money Problems

The first card is on top. The second card is to the left on the second row. The third card is to the right on the second row. The fourth card is under the second card on the third row. The fifth card is under the third card on the third row. The sixth card is under the first card on the fourth row. The first card represents the source of the problem. The second card represents, what the questioner should do about it. The third card represents negative things working against the questioner about the problem. The fourth card represents positive things working for the questioner about the problem. The fifth card represents who has the ability to help the questioner. And the sixth card represents the final conclusion.
Stuck and Can't Move Forward

If you are having a problem, this spread can help you look at your life and figure out what can be done to make it better.

The first card is in the first row. Cards two, three, four, five, and six are on the second row starting from left to right. Cards seven and eight are on the third row from left to right. Cards nine, ten, eleven, and twelve are on the fourth row from left to right.

Cards thirteen, fourteen and fifteen are on the fifth row from left to right. And the sixteenth card is by itself on the sixth row. The first card represents how the questioner feels about their life. The second card represents how the questioner's family is getting along right now. The third card represents how the questioner's friendships are going right now. The fourth card represents how the questioner's love life is going right now. The fifth card represents how the questioner's fiscal status is going right now. The sixth card represents how the questioner's job is going right now. The seventh card represents the questioner's feelings about where they live right now. The eighth card represents the questioner's relationship spiritually right now. The ninth card represents how to make their family relationships better. The tenth card represents how to make their friendships better. The eleventh card represents how to make their love life better. The twelfth card represents how to get them more money. The thirteenth card represents how to make their job better. The fourteenth card represents how to pick a better location for them to live. The fifteenth card represents how to make their religious life better. The sixteenth card represents the conclusion of any changes that they make to better their life.

Tarot is all about intuition. You can decide to follow what the cards tell you, or make choices based on the cards you choose to have a different outcome and make your own fate. Whatever you choose it is the right decision for you.

Check out Other Books by, Jean Ruffles available Exclusively on Amazon.

Psychic: Understanding Clairvoyance and Auras.

Psychic Abilities We all have.

Chapter 13: Top Ten Myths About Tarot Cards And Tarot Reading

Myth 1 - "Tarot cards can predict the future."

Predicting the future is not difficult; we can all do it. For example, if you know someone who constantly spends more than it earns and pays for it by building up the debts of credit cards, then it is not hard to predict where he's going. Or, if you know someone who is expecting a baby, you can count on experience, accurately predict that they have many months of lack of sleep and fatigue in advance. Tarot cards do a little more. It has centuries of human experience distilled into a simple philosophy and meaning of each paper. Another way of looking at it is to say that the tarot cards do not make precise predictions of the future, simply allow us to catch a glimpse of some of the likely possibilities.

Myth 2 - "tarot cards come from ancient Egypt."

The first that tarot cards can be dated is the 16th century in Italy. There is no evidence that Tarot exists anywhere else in the world. Some people claim that the cards come from India or China, but this is also baseless speculation.

Myth 3 - "Acceptance of the death card means that someone dies."

Likely. The point of the symbolism of the Cards is that they represent deeper truths than life. Taking all the cards literally would lose layers of meaning and intuition. In the case of the death map of the medieval spirit, death represented an inevitable change and often a journey to a better place. The Charter represents change and evolution. However, the possibility that this sometimes means death cannot be ruled out.

Myth 4 - "Reading the pleasure of Tarot in the occultism."

There are many claims that the tarot cards have pagan, witchcraft, or shamanic roots, and some even involve tarot cards in devil worship and satanic rituals. Another common claim is that the tarot cards originated from ancient religions now forgotten. None of this is true. Tarot cards, as already mentioned, originate from medieval Italy, and the predominant cultural context of that time was Christian. The symbolism of the Cards is Christian or Jewish-A New Testament or an old one. The word "occult" means" hidden," so, in this sense, you can say that reading has something to do with magic because you are trying to reveal what is hidden.

Myth 5 - "Reading your cards will bring bad luck."

Professional readers and those experienced with cards know that it is not true, but this is often repeated. This may stem from the fact that Tarot readers avoid reading their cards. Not because she's unlucky, but because she's not effective. A good tarot reading requires three parts; the questioner, the reader, and the bridge. The reader tries to remain objective and reports to the questioner what the cards say, without any bias or desire to hear a specific message. Playing this role for your reading is difficult, if not impossible.

Myth 6 - "You must have a certain psychic ability to read tarot cards."

Most people can learn to read tarot cards to a smaller or larger extent. No psychic power is needed because all wisdom is in Maps and meanings that have been developed over the years. Actually, if we were psychics, why would you use Tarot Cards? Tarot works best when the reader drops his prejudices and feelings on the problem and leaves only the cards to speak.

Myth 7 - "No one should ever worry about their tarot package."

Some interns do not allow anyone else to touch their tarot cards. Even if they read something, they won't let the interview mix the game up on their own. In my experience, this valuable attitude comes from those who want to build themselves, and their platform will be something special. Let me see what you want. This is contrary to the spirit of the Tarot, which promotes open investigation and sharing of understanding. Allowing customers to shuffle cards helps them feel part of the process and focus on the problem in hand.

Myth 8 "Tarot cards can be used to cast spells or perform other people."

Sometimes it is considered that tarot cards can be used to keep things moving rather than predicting. To influence someone's life from afar, for good or evil. It is very far from what cards are actually, which is simple to understand. There is no reason to believe that tarot cards have a different power than intuition. One of the frequent messages based on the tarot data is, in fact, a bad ability that sometimes we have to influence our lives without talking about someone else. Just to give a tarot would probably say: "Get a grip before you try to change others."

Myth 9 - "Different bridges provide different figurines."

It's a little subjective, but not in my experience. Regardless of the bridge, the meanings obtained during the four centuries remain the same. However, different people will refer more strongly to some of the bridges, rather than the other, and the images with which the client is more comfortable to create the best atmosphere for reading. A cynical person may suspect that this myth is multiplied by the creators of bridges.

Myth 10 - "It's dangerous to have too much data on tarot cards."

There is a belief that people who become obsessed with tarot cards and continue to make one after the second reading, you're out of luck, or take a risk, push yourself over the limit. Perhaps it is true that the search for permanent help can be a sign of an impending crisis. These people could still be near the edge. The main thing is that too many tips hurt anyone and lead only to confusion.

Know All About Your Love Life Through Love Tarot Reading

Love and emotions can cloud judgments and leave you confused. It can affect other aspects of your life and get you down.

It is better to clarify issues related to love, relationship, and progress in life.

Tarot provides meaningful answers and directions to define your situation and what you can do to change the situation for the better.

Formulate specific questions and problems before going for a love tarot reading

Interestingly, experienced and gifted Tarot readers first find out what exactly your interest is and what your questions are when you approach them for the love tarot reading.

Then it exposes the number of cards in a template.

In general, you can question classified information as relating to you, love, and your love life in the future, how to find love, how to resolve conflicts, and to spread the love of the couple.

For each type, the medium tarot reader will spread the cards in a special way and invent the love of reading.

Tarot Love Spreads

In a love tarot reading, the reader can take advantage of specific spreads, which usually defines the relationship Tarot deviations, such as finding love to spread, love bottom line spread, relationship deviations, and couple reading deviations. The number of Cards selected can vary from five to twelve.

Your friendly Tarot reader will arrange tarot cards according to the problem. Then each card is read for its individual interpretation and relative to other cards that appear in the span. Each card has a related question. For example, the first card may concern why you are still free.

The second card shows you how to overcome this situation, and the third card will inform you about the positive aspect of your potential partner.

An example is the Empress's card. If it happens in your spread and stands, it represents the result, and its symbol is Venus, showing positive developments are in stock in the near future. In itself, it means one thing. The Tarot reader interprets the card, your question, and other cards, and comes up with a detailed answer.

In case the problems with love and relationship bother you, contact the tarot expert to read the Tarot of love. Knowing your wishes, the Tarot reader will arrange the game in a special way specifically for the love tarot reading session that gives you the long-awaited answers.

Using the Tarot to Find Love

Undoubtedly, the most common survey when reading tarot is about love. It often seems that true love is something that is outside of yourself; it is the external force or the act of Destiny over which we have little control. In fact, the search for love begins with ourselves. Love is a Genesis that manifests itself in our inner beings. A happy and successful relationship begins with ourselves.

The best relationships are those in which both partners find out who they are. When a person develops with a strong sense of self, his partnership will most likely blossom. With self-consciousness, a person is more able to express his feelings and establish appropriate boundaries. They know their own needs and the needs of their partners. Above all, for someone who is single, can recognize the qualities of a potential partner that will work or not.

In the individual tarot tips on Love Matters, Most Tarot readers and psychics tend to focus directly on the current energy of someone's love life. They often do not realize the influence of their own systems of belief or behavior. During a tarot reading, it is really up to the individual to ask the tarot reader or psychic to explore the topic of their level of personal development and how it can affect their love life. A good tarot reader can read it immediately. Love problems must change their orientation. Instead of asking when I would find love? Try to explore the areas that prevent you from finding love. Here are some questions that can be very useful during a love tarot reading.

1. Where are the areas I need to grow to find love?

2. What's keeping me from finding love?

3. What do I need to know about myself so that I can meet a partner?

4. What are my behaviors that affect my love life?

5. What should I think of love?

6. What areas should I change?

7. Where can I not talk?

8. What do I have to do to open myself to love?

The more you learn about yourself, the more likely you will meet the perfect love. It is important to remember that when a person uses tarot for love, tarot serves as a seer. Tarot reading is a tool of self-renewal and growth. In truth, Tarot is a tool that is available to all who wish to explore their own inner workings. This is an incredibly effective method of immersing ourselves in the deepest areas of ourselves that affect our current relationships. Tarot data will never reveal our secrets that remain out of sight.

Tarot reading serves as a guide. They are mirrors that reflect our truths. When it comes to love, tarot cards can lead us to the manifestation of our goals and dreams. They reveal our vulnerabilities and the areas that prevent us from flourishing. In a love tarot card, you can find out what affects us and highlights situations that we may have been aware of. Above all, Tarot offers us a new sense of awareness of who we are. In the end, a tarot reading can open us to love.

As for love, there is nothing like a good tarot reading. Tarot cards offer a unique perspective that illuminates the nature of our relationships. I am here to guide you on your journey, both personally and romantic. Questions about love are by far the most common questions asked when reading the tarot. However, many people are disappointed or dissatisfied. The cause of this is often the questions that are asked. The most important aspect of successful tarot reading is to ask the right questions.

The most common mistake that is made when reading the tarot is the preservation of information. People do this when they question or test the ability of a tarot reader. It is quite normal to worry when working with a new tarot reader, especially if this is the first time you will receive a reading. In these circumstances, the biggest problem is the lack of openness of mind. Unfortunately, you do not need this or that tarot reader. The retention of information can ultimately disrupt the ability of the Tarot reader.

When you get a tarot reading, the best approach is to stay open to your questions about love prepared before you start reading. A professional tarot reader understands the cards and has learned to interpret their meaning. The more accurate you will be with a tarot reader, the better it will be able to help you read. Take the time to justify yourself with doubts and let yourself be guided by the cards. You will be surprised at the amount of information you can receive when you stay recipient.

The best questions to ask at first reading love tarot should not be in black and white. In other words, asking if someone you love or if your relationship will work can give the Tarot reader very little work. Here are some examples of open-ended questions that might be useful when reading Tarot a message.

1. What affects my relationship?

2. What is touching my interest in love now?

3. How could I develop this relationship?

4. What should I understand about myself?

5. What should I understand about my interest in love?

6. What is the potential outcome of this report?

7. What should I do to bring a romantic relationship into my life?

The list can go on, and you can be as creative as you want. Asking carefully planned questions can lead to very rewarding tarot readings.

It is also wise to inform the Tarot reader about the context of your situation. This is especially true for the tarot details of love. By allowing the Tarot reader to fully understand the nature of your situation, the more they will be able to guide you.

The history of the situation often improves the Reading of tarot cards. This gives the reader a broader perspective and allows him to understand the problems he is facing. It also lets you know what has affected your relationship.

Finally, it is important to remember that a good Tarot reader will never tell you what to do. They are essentially messengers. You are your master, and you have your free will. You have the power to choose your own paths and behaviors. When it comes to love, you are always the best guide. While tarot readings can often reveal important influences, they still have the power to make their own decisions and choose their own plan of action.

Conclusion

I've decided to dedicate the last section of my book to some broad ideas about the art of tarot reading in general. As I mentioned even from the initial paragraphs of the book, the main thing that made me consider creating this beginner's guide was the widespread misleading information about this practice. For this reason, I want to emphasize the fact that my goal is, under no circumstance, that of encouraging or trying to convince anyone to start practicing tarot reading, or going more often (or for the first time) to a reader.

This book was written precisely for those who are already interested in this topic, and want to find out the truth about it (not the myths that circulate freely from generation to generation and without a definite foundation). At the same time, I wanted to create a concise presentation of the most important elements that any beginner should know. You might have observed that I omitted certain elements (reversed reading being probably the main one). The reason for doing this was the fact that I didn't want to complicate things from the beginning.

Any person who does his or her reading for the first time needs to understand exactly what each card, suit, and position means, because these are the elements that will eventually lead to the development of a personal interpretation. After setting these basic details very well in your mind, you will be able to move forward to the cards with double or more specific meanings. But for the initial phase, these should be enough. Moreover, in some cases, there is a tendency to feel constrained by too much theory, and this is exactly what you need to avoid. In the end, tarot reading depends as much on the seeker as on the reader (when they are not the same person), so you wouldn't want to deprive the person in front of you of important details because of a book.

The next step is, obviously, to try everything that you have learned for yourself. This is the only way in which you will be able to get to your own understanding of all the meanings of each card, and achieve your personal experience in tarot reading. Remember: tarot reading is not about foreseeing your future or communicating with other dimensions; it's about the unlimited power of our unconscious and what really determines all our choices, fears, and desires.

www.ingramcontent.com/pod-product-compliance
Lightning Source LLC
Chambersburg PA
CBHW071447070526
44578CB00001B/249